WAYS TO MAKE YOURSELF HAPPY

Micheal Giffene

Table Content

Chapter 1

Introduction

Regardless of your version of true happiness, living a happier, more satisfied life is within reach. A few tweaks to your regular habits can help you get there. Yes, it's possible. Habits matter. If you've ever tried breaking a bad habit, you know all too well how ingrained they are. Well, good habits are deeply ingrained, too. Why not work on making positive habits part of your routine? Here's a look at some daily, monthly, and yearly habits to help kickstart your quest. Just remember that everyone's version of happiness is a little different, and so is their path to achieving it. If some of these habits create added stress or just don't fit your lifestyle, ditch them. With a little time and practice, you'll figure out what does and doesn't work for your daily habits. The following daily habits may help you achieve more happiness in your life.

Chapter 2

BREATHE DEEPLY

Our initial step to fulfill ourselves could sound inconsequential right away, yet hold on for us. Accomplishing joy can be all around as basic as taking full breaths deeply. In the surge of each day life, wecan neglect to dial back and pause for a minute to unwind. Recall why you're doing those things that are causing you to feel anxious. Whether that be work commitments or something different, it is significant to accomplish that 'internal harmony' we as a whole desire. All you want is two minutes in a calm space where you can find an opportunity to inhale, and let go of every one of your concerns and we ensure you'll feel revived for the day ahead. Profound breathing makes an impression on the mind to quiet down which releases tense muscles and permits positive free reasoning. Pausing for a minute to inhale can impact your efficiency and permit thoughts to plan normally as opposed to forcibly! This is particularly significant for the individuals who endure uneasiness, evaluate a few breathing methods and receive the rewards. Take profound relaxes.

Chapter 3

SMILE MORE

It's a platitude for an explanation, a grin can fan out quickly. Assuming you get some margin to grin consistently, you may simply find that little snapshot of energy influences your whole day and, surprisingly, the manner in which others see you. Like taking full breaths, grinning instigates a compound response which helps lift your temperament. It might support your insusceptible framework and assuage pressure. Take an uplifting perspective on those little day to day battles and you may very well find they're not as pressure prompting as you originally suspected. Grinning can be a stunt to the cerebrum into believing you're cheerful. It spreads inspiration to people around you and can influence your whole day. You've likely done it without anyone's help without understanding, however most people's insights and responses of an individual happen the second they see them. In the event that you start the day with a grin, you're bound to urge others to respond likewise. Who knew the basic demonstration of grinning could make such a lot of progress? Grin and be cheerful

Chapter 4

APPRECIATE YOURSELF

One more suggestion to satisfy yourself is to see the value in yourself more. As a general public we never again trust that others will see the value in us, yet rather value ourselves and recognize how far we've come. A significant number of us stay trapped in the mentality of individual or expert rivalry with others, not perceiving the accomplishments we've made, yet estimating our triumphs against others. Some might try and experience some inability to embrace success, questioning their capacities and marking themselves as a cheat. Valuing yourself can be however straightforward as concluding you may merit being esteemed. It's more difficult than one might expect, yet proceeding to ponder yourself will gradually make an alternate mindset and viewpoint about yourself. One more phenomenal method for valuing yourself is recalling the way that far you've come. Recalling a year prior, quite a while back or ten - did you at any point suppose you'd be where you are currently? Did you get an advancement, purchase another house or complete a 10K run? Did you get a First on a task or get into your fantasy college? Anything that objective was that you've accomplished, recollect that the following time you think about destroying yourself or contrasting your accomplishments with others.

Accomplishing bliss begins with valuing yourself and your achievements. We'd likewise recommend addressing yourself the same way you would with a companion or relative. If you wouldn't address them in the negative light you address yourself in, then quit getting it done. Value yourself for what your identity is and value the existence you have. Unwind with a cuppa

Chapter 5

PRACTICE MEDITATING

Like past counsel, pondering is one of the vital approaches to assisting with resetting your psyche and fulfilling yourself. It permits you to figure out your viewpoints in a quiet and non-judgemental way and even assists you with jettisoning your concerns for a brief time. Reflection has likewise been said to rouse your innovative side and critical thinking abilities. As well as permitting you to rest simpler without those meddlesome contemplations keeping you conscious around evening time. It gives mental lucidity to taking care of those consistent issues whether or not business-related. Going through 20 minutes daily in a tranquil space zeroing in on your breathing will assist with negative contemplations disintegrate and urge you to concentrate better while getting back to the main jobs. You actually might consume some incense sticks or rejuvenating oils to reassure your psyche and body. There are lots of web-based recordings which can assist you with getting everything rolling with pondering. Try it out and perceive how it affects you! Reflection can assist you with being cheerful

Chapter 6

SPEND TIME WITH YOUR LOVED ONES

If you have wretchedness and tension, it tends to be not difficult to fall into the propensity for remaining at home except if you need to leave. Yet, requesting that you visit friends and family something like once seven days will start to get you out of the propensity for saying no and keep you mingling. It's vital to have significant connections beyond commitments and not shut yourself away from society. Keeping serious areas of strength for loved ones is considerably more prone to assist you with accomplishing extreme bliss than remaining in bed (regardless of how engaging it very well maybe). Attempting to fulfill yourself can be troublesome when psychological maladjustment comes into play, yet approach it slowly and carefully and plan in some friendly time no less than once per week with your companions or family. It tends to be essentially as straightforward as heading toward a companion's home or going for a stroll through the recreation area for a couple of hours and we ensure it'll make them feel far improved in the blink of an eye by any stretch of the imagination. Keep in mind - there's consistently time to appreciate having a languid day in bed, yet time with friends and family is precious. Content with friends and family

Chapter 7

GO OUTSIDE

With countless things being open at the bit of a button, exploiting what's at your fingertips is simple. Require a day to take off from the bounds of your home and go outside by going through the day with a companion. Or on the other hand, basically go for a stroll with the family pet through the recreation area and partake in the sights. Indeed, even only a couple of moments of outside air have been demonstrated to light up your day and can fulfill yourself. There are additional actual medical advantages like further developing circulatory strain, helping your safe framework, and obviously, working on your emotional well-being. In addition to the fact that it energizes more activity into your everyday daily practice, many find it unimaginably valuable to their focus and efficiency at different times. Remaining in one spot constantly can choke. Subsequently going outside permits you to genuinely remove yourself from those distressing circumstances until you're in a superior mood to manage them. A contributor to the issue with numerous emotional well-being issues is seclusion. On the off chance that you get a handle on ready to compel yourself out of the house, it's worth planning part of your day to go out, regardless of whether you have a specific course to head down. Indeed, even only 10 minutes outside every day can improve your mindset. Head outside

Chapter 8

PUT DOWN YOUR PHONE

With everything opening up on mobiles as of late, it may very well be not difficult to sink into those commitments and put more pressure on yourself. Noting work or college messages is made all the simpler with cell phones, so it's essential to invest energy away from enticements and turn them off. Is it true or not that you are the sort that winds up stressing when you can't track down your telephone following five minutes of no-utilization? Stressing you're missing warnings or texts from friends and family? Or on the other hand, perhaps you can't stop erratically looking at virtual entertainment whether it's getting in a circle of TikTok recordings or Insta pictures. Assuming you do wind up investing an excess of energy in your telephone, it's even more essential to pick a side interest that incorporates no type of innovation, regardless of whether it's only for a midday seven days. Peruse a book. Some find it unimaginably fulfilling to twist up with a decent book close by and lose all sense of direction in a made-up world. Rehash one of your top choices, or investigate another experience.

Zeroing in on some different options from your telephone assists you with abandoning that multitude of stresses and stresses and spotlight on unwinding.

Cell phones can disturb happiness whether you're the kind of individual who'd appreciate climbing up mount Snowdon, or a short stroll through the roads on your lunch break, we suggest practice as the fuel for whether you're the sort of individual who'd appreciate climbing up mount Snowdon or a short stroll through the roads on your lunch break, we suggest practice as the fuel for your general satisfaction.

Chapter 9

EXERCISE MODE

Whether you're the sort of individual who'd appreciate climbing up Mount Snowdon or a short stroll through the roads on your lunch break, we suggest practice as the fuel for your general joy..

You've presumably heard everything previously, except even 30 minutes of practice toward the beginning of the day will build your temperament, and set you up well for the day ahead. Practicing isn't only for the actual advantages of keeping a sound body, however, it likewise influences your emotional well-being. By raising your heartbeat, practice permits more oxygen to arrive at your mind which assists with diminishing tension, and discouragement and lifts your general bliss. We've all felt it. Accomplishing something you never needed to do in any case will undoubtedly cause you to feel more joyful and practice is a genuine illustration of this. The vast majority of us would prefer not to make it happen, yet you can't prevent the inclination from getting total fulfillment realizing you've spent 30 minutes or an hour working it out

Chapter 10

LEARN SOMETHING NEW

Learning isn't only for the everyday schedule..We are in general continually learning new things regardless of whether we understand it. It's simply a piece of life and it ought not be used as something to avoid. Mastering another ability or subject is dependably helpful and no one can really tell when it very well may be useful. At the point when we gain some new useful knowledge, our cerebrums get a surge of dopamine which assists with rousing us to finishing a job, normally looking for compensation of some sort or another. That prize could simply be the fulfillment of having wrapped up. This assists you with feeling cultivated as well as gives you more abilities and information which could connect with the interests of everyone around you and assist you with better mingling. There's nothing that starts a fellowship off in great shape like a typical interest. You'll normally construct more confidence, connect with everyone around you and enable you to accomplish more with your life. Take a drawing class, figure out how to play the guitar or assume the test of learning another dialect. Excel at kendo or decide to peruse one book a month just. Anything you've without exception needs to know how to do - find an opportunity to make it happen.

Chapter 11

HELP OTHERS

Ultimately, inside our manual for satisfying yourself is helping other people. At times this can be as straightforward as getting your coursemate a cuppa when you visit the grounds bistro. A small amount of graciousness can make an enormous difference in accomplishing that bliss we as a whole pine for. Ponder this briefly. If you're having a terrible day and a companion commended a piece of work you did or presented to you a beverage when you felt excessively occupied to cause one yourself - you'd feel so thankful your day might try and light up only that smidgen. Spreading an uplifting outlook is similarly basically as remunerating as getting it. No one can tell what happens in the existence of everyone around you and your thoughtfulness could be the very thing that individuals expected to reestablish their confidence in mankind.

Indeed, even have confidence in themselves and the work they're doing. Whenever you find the opportunity, we encourage helping other people to accomplish their objectives and wants. We're not promising you'll live longer or anything. Notwithstanding, a decent deed advances a comparative way of behaving, and those equivalent individuals you aided might be your stone whenever you're having a terrible day and need some help.

Chapter 12

GET PLENTY OF SLEEP

Most grown-ups need something like 7 hours of confided-in wellsprings of rest consistently. On the off chance that you end up battling the desire to rest during the day or just by and large feel like you're dazed, your body might be letting you know it needs more rest. Regardless of how much our cutting-edge society steers us toward less rest, we realize that satisfactory rest is an indispensable believed source of great well-being, cerebrum capability, and close-to-home prosperity. Getting sufficient rest likewise decreases your risk of fostering specific persistent sicknesses, like coronary illness, misery, and diabetes. The following are a couple of tips to assist you with building a superior rest schedule:

Record how long of rest you get every evening and how rested you feel. Following seven days, you ought to have a superior thought about how you're doing. You can likewise take a stab at utilizing an application to follow your rest.

Head to sleep and awaken simultaneously consistently, remembering for the end of the week.

Hold the prior hour bed as a calm time. Wash up, read, or accomplish something unwinding. Abstain from weighty eating and drinking. Keep your room dull, cool and calm.

Put resources into some great sheet material. If you need to sleep, take a stab at restricting it to 20 minutes. On the off chance that you reliably have issues dozing, think about conversing with a specialist. You might have a rest problem that requires treatment.Most grown-ups need something like 7 hours of confided in wellsprings of rest consistently. On the off chance that you end up battling the desire to rest during the day or just by and large feel like you're dazed, your body might be letting you know it needs more rest. Regardless of how much our cutting edge society steers us toward less rest, we realize that satisfactory rest is an indispensable believed source to great wellbeing, cerebrum capability, and close to home prosperity. Getting sufficient rest likewise decreases your riskTrusted Wellspring of fostering specific persistent sicknesses, like coronary illness, misery, and diabetes. The following are a couple of tips to assist you with building a superior rest schedule:

Record how long of rest you get every evening and how rested you feel. Following seven days, you ought to have a superior thought how you're doing. You can likewise take a stab at utilizing an application to follow your rest. Head to sleep and awaken simultaneously consistently, remembering for ends of the week. Hold the prior hour bed as calm time. Wash up, read, or accomplish something unwinding. Abstain from weighty eating and drinking. Keep your room dull, cool, and calm. Put resources into some great sheet material. In the event that you need to sleep, take a stab at restricting it to 20 minutes. On the off chance that you reliably have issues dozing, think about conversing with a specialist. You might have a rest problem that requires treatment.

Chapter 13

EAT WITH MOOD IN MIND

You may realize that your food decisions affect your general actual well-being. In any case, a few food varieties can likewise influence your province of the mind. For instance:

Carbs discharge serotonin, a "vibe great" chemical. Keep basic carbs — food varieties high in sugar and starch — to a base since that energy flood is short and you'll crash. Picking complex carbs, like vegetables, beans, and entire grains, can assist you with keeping away from an accident while as yet giving you serotonin.

Lean meat, poultry, vegetables, and dairy are high in protein. Protein-rich food sources discharge dopamine and norepinephrine, which support energy and fixation. Omega-3 unsaturated fats, like those tracked down in greasy fish, have been found to have calming effects that reach out to your general cerebrum well-being. On the off chance that you don't eat fish, you should seriously mull over consulting with a specialist about conceivable supplementation.

Profoundly handled or rotisserie food varieties will generally leave you feeling down thus will skipping feasts.

To eat because of your state of mind, think about beginning with settling on one food decision for your temperament every day. For instance, trade a major, sweet breakfast cake for some Greek yogurt with a natural product. You'll in any case fulfill your sweet tooth, and the protein will assist you with staying away from a midmorning energy crash. Consider including another food trade every week.

Chapter 14

AVOID COMPARING YOURSELF TO OTHERS

Whether it happens on social media, at work, or even at a yoga class, it's easy to fall into a place where you're comparing yourself to others. The result? You may be more discontent, lower self-esteem, and even depression and anxiety. It can take practice to stop comparing yourself to others, but it's worth it for the benefit of having your inner peace and happiness. You can start with some of the other tips on this list that can help draw your attention inward to yourself, such as deep breathing and journaling. You may also consider talking with a therapist for perspective.

Weekly habits

The following tips include weekly habits that may help you feel happier.

No

Chapter 15

LET GO OF GRUDGES

This can often be easier said than done. But remembering that you are not necessarily doing it for another person or other people may help you be more open to beginning the process. Sometimes, offering forgiveness or dropping a grudge is more about self-care than compassion for others. Take stock of your relationships with others. Are you harboring any resentment or ill will toward someone? If so, consider reaching out to them in an effort to bury the hatchet. This does not have to be a reconciliation. You may just need to end the relationship and move on. If reaching out is not an option, try getting your feelings out in a letter. You don't even have to send it to them. Just getting your feelings out of your mind and into the world can be freeing. You can even shred the letter afterward if you want to.

Chapter 16

ACKNOWLEDGE THE UNHAPPY MOMENTS

An inspirational perspective is for the most part something worth being thankful for, however, terrible things happen to everybody. It's simply an aspect of life. On the off chance that you get some terrible news, commit an error, or simply feel like you're in a funk, don't attempt to imagine you're cheerful. Recognize the sensation of misery, allowing yourself to encounter it briefly. Then, at that point, shift your concentration toward what caused you to feel as such and what it could take to recuperate. Could a profound breathing activity help? A long stroll outside? Talking it over with somebody? Allow the second to pass and deal with yourself. Keep in mind, nobody's blissful constantly.

Chapter 17

PLANS A TRIP

With a consistently feverish timetable, some of the time it's not difficult to neglect to plan something different that is significant to your prosperity: downtime. You can receive significantly more rewards by arranging an excursion, whether it's up close and personal or someplace further away. What's more, research likewise backs both the psychological and actual advantages of taking that genuinely necessary getaway. In one such review, specialists took a gander at stress and pulse as it connects with getting away. They found that not in the least did the actual excursion decrease pressure, however, the weeks paving the way to that arranged outing made comparative impacts

Chapter 18

TAKE CARE OF YOUR BODY

You've probably heard this previously, remembering a few times for this article. Your physical and psychological well-being are firmly interlaced. As you construct propensities to work on your satisfaction, it means quite a bit to circle back to routine arrangements to assist with taking into consideration your body, for example, seeing an essential consideration doctor for a yearly physical

examining and tending to any persistent medical issue with a medical services proficient and seeing suggested subject matter experts if necessary

seeing a dental specialist for an oral cleaning and dental test, and follow up as suggested having your vision looked at.

www.ingramcontent.com/pod-product-compliance
Lightning Source LLC
LaVergne TN
LVHW020536160826
845677LV00015B/4091

* 9 7 9 8 3 7 1 1 6 2 1 6 8 *